Reclaiming the Nectar and the Hum

Peg Edera

Fernwood
PRESS

Reclaiming the Nectar and the Hum

©2025 by Peg Edera

Fernwood Press
Newberg, Oregon
www.fernwoodpress.com

All rights reserved. No part may be reproduced for any commercial purpose by any method without permission in writing from the copyright holder.

Printed in the United States of America

Cover and page design: Mareesa Fawver Moss
Cover art: Ruslan Sikunov via Unsplash

ISBN 978-1-59498-166-1

Peg Edera's powerful new collection *Reclaiming the Nectar and the Hum* is a book that begins with one wish and becomes a murmuration of wishes for past, present, and future generations. It is a book that takes flight, opening its pages like wings and lifting us up poem by poem to see the possibility of a new creation—a mended, reclaimed creation flying the banner of love. "Yes, yes, All of this," these healing poems say to us. Edera's book beats with a brave heart. Read it and feel that beautiful pulse all around you.

—Annie Lighthart
author of *Pax*

Peg Edera's courageous and beautiful poems move with and beyond grief—the death of an infant daughter, a mother's long neglect—to become songs like "exhales of prayers." In her poems, we encounter the luminous and the reclaimed, rooting ourselves in new, engendering ground filled with possibility. She dares us to "keep... eyes open to the chance of gleam." Unabashedly, her poems seek to find a kind of dogged hope, framing the everyday world in a renewed attention like "the drifting scent of wild roses/ faded dish towels flapping on a line." Immersed in her generous world, I feel reassured, listening for "the world's hum rising." I am ready to "believe that everything has an angel."

—Andrea Potos
author of *Her Joy Becomes* and *Marrow of Summer*

Peg Edera's poetry is a north star for daughters who are reconciling the journey they travel with their mothers from birth to afterlife and back again. Throughout the manuscript, Edera offers a series of delicate imprints, wisdom "wrapped in cornhusks" and angel wings. She writes of beauty as an identity to be recognized and grief as a labyrinth to be honored with loving kindness. "If only we pay attention/ if only we slow down..." Edera invites the reader to parse moments of life, to taste the honeysuckle nectar, to pay attention, to sing an aria of mothers, daughters. *Reclaiming the Nectar and the Hum* is an invitation to remember dreams that have been set aside amid a maternal journey of "following our hearts."

—Gwendolyn Morgan
author of *Flight Feathers*

In 2018, I read Peg Edera's book *Love Is Deeper Than Distance*, poems which brought into focus living life with her husband Fred, who, at the relatively young age of sixty-five, was struck with dementia and then soon after, ALS. Fred died at sixty-seven. In my testimonial, I wrote, "At the living core of this work is openness to loving." I was moved by Peg's capacity to stay with Fred throughout a harrowing experience. Now, five years later, I have in my possession another book of poems by Peg, and I am happy to say that these poems are an expression of an openness to living. The emotional range and concern of these poems is broader than loving. You will find poems that reflect the shadow-side of life. Peg's fun, natural turbulence, reclaiming her life—the nectar and hum—is given room to play. In these poems, she stays with herself. Many poems have a particular gravity—they orbit and then land within the fraught and blessed relationship between mother and daughter. Reading them, you will appreciate this line from "Advice I Wish My Mother Had Given Me": "Learn to speak your own language." Peg is doing that. I encourage you to join her.

—JOHN FOX
author of *Poetic Medicine: The Healing Art of Poem-Making*

To Mia and Annalee, of course and always

Contents

A Birthday Wish 10
No More Imprint But My Own 11
I Thought You Were Dead 12
Please 14
How to Survive 16
Unburying Angels 18
Bench 19
If I Was a Shameless Hussy 20
What a Mother Says 22
More Precious Than My Mother's Pearls 24
One More Thing I Never Thought to Ask About 25
Makeup 27
After All These Years I Still Can't
    Believe You Bought That Plot 28
The Best Solution to Some Days Is to Forget Them. 29
What Made Me Think I Have the Courage for This? ... 30
Baptism 32
The Hum 34
Cemetery September 2019 35
What I Really Want to Say 36
Begin Again 37

The Risk You Take for Better	38
How To Sing an Aria	39
Nectar	40
Five Wishes	41
So Much Depends on the Frame	42
Do You Remember	43
Advice I Wish My Mother Had Given Me	45
Migration Story	47
Things I Love—A Counting Poem	49
On the Seventh Anniversary of Her Sister's Death	50
One More September Poem	51
Sometimes You Have a Friend	52
Thirty-One	54
My Garden	55
After the Van Gogh Immersion	56
Wedding Ring	57
For Lack of a Metaphor	58
How to End Narcissism	60
Heart	62
Notes from *A Distant Mirror*	63
Let Me Give Thanks	64
Sunday Dinner with My Daughter	65
One Piece of Broken Pottery	67
Blessing	68
To Have Faith	69
Awake in the Night	70
Screaming Without Sound	72
Let Our Anarchy Be First	73
Daughters, Listen	74
Live the Life that Chooses You	76
Who Held You Through the Terrible Night?	77
Daughter of the Falling Star	79
Acknowledgments	81
Title Index	83
First Line Index	87

Respecting the storm
be slow to tell the story.
It will be a long time
before all that has passed
washes ashore.

A Birthday Wish

Someday, I hope,
she will read my poems
and know me as I never knew
my mother.
Maybe these poems
can reroute the mother roads
this family follows.
A tall order for little words
strung together in patterns even I
sometimes don't see.
A tall order for what happens
when I follow the maze of my mind
to the bench between hedges and find
what I really want to say.
I dream this dream for my daughter.
I do not want her to wake on her birthday
in her wiser years
to realize she will
always be lonely
because her mother was someone
she couldn't know.

No More Imprint But My Own

I am no longer my father's thing,
my mother's servant.

Those days of daughter went with them
to their very own places of repair
which is what happens to the broken at death.

I am no longer the wife—
one divorce, one death,

and those imprints are lifted
like a big seal pumped up by hydraulic jack
high enough I slipped from beneath.

Arthritis slipped the seal of work,
and arthritis is not an imprint.

It is more like a harsh harness only, I think,
death will remove.
Unless my assumptions are wrong.

I could be widow, but it is
more a fact now than an imprint.

Mother is no longer an imprint.
It is a contract I sign every day.
Poet is a personal choice as is friend.

Your imprint—which you offer vaguely hoping
I might try it on like a hat and we can see how it fits—

I'm not accepting it
even when I am lonely
like a person behind closed curtains and locked doors.

I think my days of imprint are over.
It's all choice from here on out.

I Thought You Were Dead

If your mother knocked on your door
with a wide willow basket in her arms
and she, who you knew as dead these many years, said
This is for you. Inside are all the answers I have,
would you slam the door and throw the bolt?
Would you hesitate? Would you throw open the door?
Burst into tears, the waters of your breached dam
flooding the room?

What I would do is this:
Dry-eyed and a little breathless, I'd say
Well, this is unexpected.
I bet I have more questions
than you have answers.
I'd say, *Why now, Mom?*
I'd say, *Good to see you, sort of.*
Why did you let him
do that to us?
I'd say, *What happened to you*
that twisted you like a gnarled tree
overgrown with briars?
What didn't you get that you needed?
Who failed you?
What kept you so far from your treasure?
What cloud covered your North Star?
What rain never stopped flooding your river?

And she wouldn't say a word.
She'd place the basket by the door
and walk away.

Inside, wrapped in cornhusks,
I'd find a doll.
Her face a little wizened apple.
Her hair gray moss.
Her gingham apron colorless with age
and her heart still bleeding
cherry juice that drips
down my arm.

Please
for Rosie

Grandmothers,

could you teach us how to be
brave enough for this lifetime?

We could learn to save the moments
you send us in a bravery bank.

Like the moments of sun and light
mixing up into an elixir of strength.

Like a tree banks light all summer,
storing it bravely in her roots all winter.

We'd bottle the elixir in amber bottles
sealed with pine green wax.

Store it in the old trunk
with leather straps

we'd rub with sandalwood oil.
The trunk we keep behind the wall

that opens when we push the third brick
from the left of the painting

of you all sitting in a circle
with the stars bright above you.

We'd do that faithfully.
We'd take it on like religion

if you could tell us,
grandmothers,

how much we need for this lifetime
and where we find more
when we're running out.

How to Survive

Check your breathing.
Still happening?
Stay with it.

Close your eyes if you need to.
If not, open them wider,
more light is good.

Notice one thing—
give it all the words you can find
even if it is a scrap of lint or a crumpled piece of paper.
Words ground us.

Remember you are smarter than they think,
no matter what proof they've got.
You have your own intelligence.
What is it you really know?
At the moment maybe it is only that they are wrong.
Good, start there.

Hum.
There is a way to hum silently.
You can practice it,
or hum so you can hear it.
Humming is a small form of yes.
Humming is a way to call to everything
that is underneath the hard stuff.

Cry. Then make a choice.
Even if it is the choice to keep crying,
choose it. You are in charge for this moment.

Listen for something you like.
Keep listening until you find something.
You will.

Leave.
If you can't walk out the door,
imagine walking out the door.

Remember:
soon some small good thing will show up.
Look for it.
Then look for the next.

Unburying Angels

Not all angels are winged.

Be faithful
to that glittering speck under the storm's debris.

Keep your eyes open to the chance of gleam.

Don't give up.

Remember you are stronger than you think.

Believe that everything has an angel—
>   even yourself
>   no matter how deeply buried.

Angels like to be found,
>   so dig deep, keep digging.

Once unburied there is soaring—
>   pay attention, it is not what you expect.

Remember your expectations are clouds and veils.
>   Step out from behind them—
>   you'll see more angels.

It's okay to talk to them. Ask for help.
>   Listen closely to their voices in the wind,
>   the leaf rustle, the birds,
>   the wind chimes, waterfall.

People will not always believe you.
>   Be gentle with their doubts.

Bench

On a rusted metal tag
on the back of the bench,

under the sycamore
at the lip of the park:

*Mother, we will sit here
and think of you.*

I imagine everyone who sits here
and reads the tag

thinks of their mother
and sighs, smiles

or twitches
as though to shake off cobwebs.

Every mother memory
brings its own smell,

the private passing scent
of yeast or violets,

cigarette smoke,
Chanel #5, Ivory soap.

Maybe some who sit here
read the tag
and do not return.

If I Was a Shameless Hussy

If I was a shameless hussy,
I'd tell you how

I made those boys-almost-men fall
like big timber in a dark forest,

how I knew to be a little
smarter than they were used to

but not so smart they felt dumb,
how I knew to look at them

like I knew them better
than anyone else and they were worthy,

how I could shine what light I had
on them, so they thought I was the sun.

If I was a shameless hussy,
I'd ignore completely
the hussy part.
I'd throw it out
with the coffee grounds and chicken bones.
I'd redact it from the dictionaries
and my mother's mouth.

It's the shameless part I'd hold onto.
I'd wear it
like a Girl Scout badge
earned on a windy canoe trip
with hard portages across mountains.
I'd be the girl that never looked back and just kept going. I'd let
shameless be a full gospel choir in my head
telling me I was walking on holy ground.

I'd be shameless and kind.
I'd stitch those words together into
a black lace bra.

So here's to reclamation projects
and staking my ground
flying the black lace banner.

What a Mother Says

Get over it

What did you expect?

Don't cry over spilt milk

Your face is like a horse

Geography never solved anything

You can do better or maybe you can't

Just say thank you

Straighten up and fly right

I'll say no for you if you can't

I told you so

Who do you think you are?

Hells bells

I'm going to slap you

   —Regeneration—

I'd fix it for you if I could

Oh Honey

Sit on my lap, I'll read to you

Look! Wait!

I'm right here with you

Let's have tea

Let's go shopping

Let's go to the beach

I know you loved him

I'm so glad you are safe

Come home for as long as you want

Bring your friends

What do you want for supper

You're the candles on the cake

I remember

Your dad loved you more than anything

More Precious Than My Mother's Pearls

I'd like to discover a book
my mother wrote advice in.
It would be more precious
than her strand of pearls
or the pin of little garnets
shaped like a star.

Now I want that book she didn't write.
It would be small, thin, worn
blue leather, the ink faded,
the penmanship precise and pretty,
every Y perfectly looped.
I can't find it, and she's been dead for twenty-five years.
I'm running out of hope
that it will turn up.

Next week I'll go to the beach cabin—
the one where my feet are always bare.
They remember all the summers
she'd shoo us out the door early
until we'd straggle back for lunch
on the porch, sandy feet sprayed off,
wet bathing suits peeled down by the back door,
little naked girls eating tuna sandwiches
on white bread with sweet pickles,
not thinking for a split second
we'd someday spend our hot afternoons looking
for the book she didn't write that told us
we'd be moonstruck by our mistakes,
baffled by our children,
hormones would swamp us like the tide surges,
and when our feet ache, hot sand,
hot sand up to our ankles—
that's the best.

One More Thing I Never Thought to Ask About

A sterling silver salamander
slithered on her lapel,
almost a snake
except for four little feet.
Staring at it,
almost mesmerized,
it didn't occur to me then,
before I came to her waist,
what an odd piece of jewelry it was.
I've never heard anyone say
I want a newt on my collar.

After she died
it emerged from her jewelry box,
a lost artifact from a tomb of memories.
More inclined to wearing pins than my sister,
it went in my pile
along with the silver parrot
with the red bead eye.

These pins seem of an age
when they were real gifts,
not cheap stuff.
I wonder who gave them to her?
Not my father.
His best ever might have been
a sweater set, though not cashmere.
Did her mother buy it for her birthday
or as a consolation for disappointments?
Or was it one of her pre-Dad conquests
at a loss for words but not for cash?

Maybe she bought it for herself
after reading the Chinese folklore
of baby dragons, symbols of luck,
of regeneration after trauma.
If only it had worked.

Makeup

My mother's lipstick was bright red,
cherry red, fire engine red.
It went on early,
was reapplied all day,
into the night.
I wonder if her lips were dyed
by all the glossy stuff
screwed up from the
depths of a golden tube,
her red lips that never seemed to fade
on that face framed by almost-black hair,
graying hair, gray hair
with dark eyes full of jokes and ridicule
and sadness.
A sadness, I see now,
she tried to hide
coming in as inevitable as a tide.
Those red lips around a white cigarette,
those lips reflected in the mirror
mashing together, ready
for one more application.
Those red lips
on napkins and Kleenex,
sitting triumphant on her face
even from her hospital bed
that last minute.
They were just as she liked them.

After All These Years I Still Can't Believe You Bought That Plot

A little crock of her ashes
lies under polished red granite
right beside my first daughter
and my husband.
Shrugging my shoulders,
that universal posture of whatever,
I visit them all now
even though I don't want to visit her.

I clean the stones, leave flowers.
A smaller one for her.
I say, Hi, Mom.
I tell her it's the best I can do for her.

As a general rule, I try not to lie,
but I don't tell her I can't believe
she bought this plot
in these verdant, willow-draped,
rolling hills of the dead,
right beside Annalee and Fred.
I don't show her the posture
of Edvard Munch's *Scream*—
the one that always starts these visits.

I know there is a lesson in acceptance here,
of you, who gave me
the gift of all gifts.
I know you are worthy
of my compassion, my curiosity,
but when I come here—
I only cry for them.

The Best Solution to Some Days Is to Forget Them.

The art of learning to forget
is underestimated and unacknowledged,
and I lift it up now.
Way, way up
because the things I've forgotten—
it's so right they
remain that way.
The joy of forgetting
is kin to the capacity
to carry on.
It's kin to the ability
to fall asleep wherever you are.

Now that I am approaching
the on-ramp to seventy,
forgetting is suspect.
It's like the front lawn of the care home.
Nevertheless, I raise it up
because it's a serious skill
when you can take denial and shame out,
separate them, and just
thank God for forgetting
all that stuff
in the middle of lilacs
and daffodils, spears of gladioli,
buttercups and those little blue flowers—
what are they called?
Oh, right,
forget-me-nots.

What Made Me Think I Have the Courage for This?

This is the question that comes to each of us
at the first slippery, squalling, milk-spurting moment.

We learn to shut that question away, lock it down
tight because the next sentence could be
I don't.

You lock it away because the better tide rolls in
as you realize this little foot

is the size of your thumb
and too soft for pebbles, thorns, or—

heaven forbid—glass. Anything it takes
to save that precious sole,

you'll swear to it until you can't
resist her desire to run.

But what this really is about is black holes.

The very first picture of a black hole was revealed today.
A collaboration of 200 scientists believing

that nature wants to be beautiful—
they even said that at the press conference.

They trained all their mighty telescopes
on one place in the universe known as M87

and showed us, tiny dustlings of the universe,
a picture of what they thought was unseeable

containing the mass of 6.5 billion suns
from 50 million light years away.

So I ask
what makes me think I have the courage for this?

And I go back to that little foot
of my five-pound daughter
delivered into my care,
and I think,
how can I not?

Baptism

For Chris, Laura and Freya

When you return to your home
with your wonderful new daughter,
    go down to the shore
    on the night of the next new moon,
    wade out to your knees
    into the dark water
    that laps against your legs
    in the same rhythm
    you pat her back.
Start with a few drops on her forehead—
    aim for the spot between her eyebrows,
    that spot they say is a door
    opening on the vast dimensions
    we often pretend don't exist.
Then, a drop or two in each open palm,
    soothe it into her tender skin whispering,
    Yes, yes, all of this,
    anoint the soles of her feet saying,
    Water for your roots to grow deep.
If she cries, let them ring out—
    here's her voice,
    the one we all will need.
Then kiss her heart.
Kiss her mother's heart.
Her mother can kiss both your hearts,
the benediction of love everlasting.

Later when the moon is full,
    go again to the shore,
    the edge that is the blessing
    of water, earth, and air.

This time bless yourselves,
   the parents
   under this holy light
   in this salt water—
   feel the sand shift beneath your feet,
   say

Yes, yes, all of this

The Hum

We think it is the sound of distant traffic,
the absence of rock and roll.
Maybe it is the hum of the furnace before it clicks on,
the ambient white noise
of computers, phones, and microwaves.

Stop bringing your keen mind to this.
When you hear a bird sing, do you leap
to name it robin, sparrow, wren?
Do you pin it to the board, label it,
move on before the ink dries?

Stop.
This an exercise in parsing moments.
It's a dip into the fountain of faith.

Listen.
It is the sound that circles the earth
in search of star song.
The one that moves the sea,
tumbles the cliffs.
It is the one the birds sing to,
calling up the sun.
The angel choir.
The heartbeat.
It's the question whale song answers.
It's the long lope of coyote.

Listen.
Raindrops on the little pond.
The reaching of scarlet runner beans.
The feel of moss, the bend of fern.
The scent of mint, the hue of lilacs.

Cemetery September 2019

I lie on the hill above their stones,
the sadness seeps into the earth
until I am just sad,
not heavy, fractious, distressed
until I can let it be
like feathers on a bird.

What I Really Want to Say

Look up.
Take a shower.

Put on your new eyes,
the ones that see past.

There is magic here—
    that's what I want to say—
it's not gone.

Without it,
it's just fear.

With it,
it's all beams and motes

of hope,
it's ferns that move like hair,

it's barking dogs learning to speak,
that are speaking,

it's the huge hum filling the silence,
the silky wrapping of air

around your ankles.

Let's all breathe
into those spaces between our ribs.

Let our hearts expand to fill
the space we make.

Begin Again

Start anywhere.
It doesn't matter,
a start's a start.
The baby does it.
The first kiss, too.

Let the courage rise in you
like a pot of water starting to boil—
you've got the water,
now give it some heat.
That's what the heart lends—
what's more than strong or brave or motivation.

You can say
Heart, add a pinch of salt to my bravery,
sunflower seeds to my strength.
It can be an incantation,
a chant the heart can move to.

Dance around the kitchen of your need—
your kitchen will never be the same again,
the cookbooks will change their exactness,
the counters will be sticky, dripping eggs and honey,
the dishes will pile in the sink, blue bowl nestled with yellow,
green plate, resting wooden spoons.
The floor will get gritty with spilled spices
and oh, the fragrance—
cinnamon and rising yeast,
sugar, garlic,
marjoram, and lavender,
all covered in the golden dust of turmeric.

Now you have made a feast of your life.
Invite your friends.
Begin again.

The Risk You Take for Better

Sometimes after a hard conversation
when the trust between you could wreck

on the shoals of inadequate words,
the waters calm,

the sea becomes a lake,
the lake becomes your calm blood.

You remember that this
is the risk you take for better.

Better, not best,
is the mountaintop today.

For now it is where you rest
knowing the best of everything changes—

the green trees brown,
the spring-fed creek dries to mud,

morning light gives way to darkness,
sleeping babies wake to squall,

the lithe body thickens,
the calm lake churns with storm—

here we go again,
moving on to better

if we remember
to dip our oars and pull.

How To Sing an Aria

What if I really got it?

    The likelihood of anything in this life in this world

being what it is?

    The chance of the robin singing to me this morning

emerged from a tiny turquoise egg?

    The odds that this red rug from Turkey rests under my feet

so far from its makers' hands and place and time?

    And wildest yet that you my daughter

        arrived just as you are

like a mandala still being drawn,

    and we share the smallest invisible things?

What if I really got it?

    Would I be able to sing arias?

        Would I be able to jump over trees?

            Would I be able to spread love

                like pollen blown from pines in spring?

Nectar

Let me give you soft pillows
   and softer blankets.
Hot cocoa with cinnamon
      and a dash of cayenne.
An inverted rainbow as a hammock
         where you are the pot of gold.
After a long drought of touch,
      the arms that encircle.
A whisper—You will be all right—
       that echoes all night long.
The dog to rest your head against,
         heartbeats by the fire.
Your tired heart will get courage.
           Your duty-bound mind, leaps of
          knowing.
Your weary eyes, bright wonder.
            Your searching ears,
the quiet songs of wisdom,
   and on your lips, sips of honeysuckle
               nectar,
       always nectar.

Five Wishes

If I had five wishes,
I'd, of course, first
wish for five more,
and out of every five,
because I will repeat that first wish,
I'd give one wish away.
Eventually the world would be
so full of wishes, we could
see them popping into being
or flowing across the sky,
a murmuration of wishes.
Second wish
a backpack full of an endless supply of poems
handwritten on scraps of paper.
I'd wander old trails and potholed
asphalt roads, I'd climb
stairs of office buildings leaving them behind me.
I'd be the Johnny Appleseed of poetry,
faithful these seeds would grow strong,
feed souls.
Third,
I'd be my cat for one day.
Enough said about that.
Fourth,
my father would tell me the truth.
All of it.
Fifth,
I'd learn to finally sing well.
I'd sing the Song of Mothers
to my daughter.
The one I always sing,
but now I would sing it loud.
It would echo in her heart.
Then I'd start again.

So Much Depends on the Frame

The lurid purple and yellow fingerpaint
framed in darker purple
makes what might have been one scrap
in a pile of kindergarten show-and-tell
a lasting monument to a mother's noticing,
a lasting monument to a child's
unintentional adding to cool passing beauty
if only we pay attention,
if only we slow down   if only
we frame it   if only for an afternoon
even if we place another offering on top
       in the same frame
             tomorrow.

Do You Remember

Do you remember that June in Harpswell
in that tall, dark house
that could have been haunted,
the faded, stained wallpaper,
the single light bulb hanging over the kitchen sink,
the narrow stairs that twisted
to the landing with the faded rag rug
you tripped on every morning?
That house across from the lobster pound,
on the hilltop over the clam flats and tidepools?
Do you remember those rubber boots,
the official black ones, the island-in-Maine ones
and poking in the pools with Graham?
Spindly long Graham who
didn't talk much but matched your curiosity
hour after sunny hour?
Do you remember learning to play UNO
with Grammie Gayle,
that game we still play thirty years later
when we have a fit of nostalgia?

If you don't, I hand this to you
and hope you feel that uncomplicated joy
that only asked you
to wake up in the morning,
eat cereal on the porch,
let the day be the day,
let the place be the place,
let me watch you
and tuck this all away
into my encyclopedia of joy.
The encyclopedia is full of you,
and you, I hope, are full of it.

If you aren't, please,
let's sit down with tea,
get real quiet,
then I'll ask,
Do you remember?

Advice I Wish My Mother Had Given Me

Learn to translate everything
into your own language.

Learn to speak your own language.

Find the people who also speak this language
or find the ones who want to learn.

Find the places you don't have to whisper
unless you want to.

Find the way to build your house
with walls your heart can rest in.

It doesn't matter if you can cook, type, sing,
or ride a horse—unless you want to.

Every time you put on makeup, ask yourself why.
There are plenty of good reasons and plenty of bad.

Next time you want to say no but say yes—
forgive yourself.

It's going to happen.
Just try to do it less and less.

When you feel shame, spit it out.
Over the bridge, onto the curb, into your napkin.

It's the wrong teacher.
Spit it out. It's poison.

When you fall in love,
just do it.

Your heart will break a million times,
so let it sing when it can.

When the worst things happen,
wherever you are,
call me.
I'll come.

Migration Story

My mother followed me across the country.
The promise of grandchildren lured her here
like the oils from the glands of smaller animals
lure cougars.
For three years she came weekly
while I was at work, my daughter at home
with the nanny.
Mother would bring a dress, a book, a toy
and pester the baby for attention
that was always too short for what she needed.
Our nanny would report:

*Her perfume was so strong,
it made the baby sneeze.*

*She wanted Mia to run to her,
but she can't even walk.*

*She thinks Mia's slow.
She's not slow, she's just not a puppet.*

On the weekends I would take Mia
to visit for one more hour,
dutiful even though I always left
with a headache, a crying baby,
and a husband thinking about beer.
Once in that third year,
my mother sharply asked Mia to come here.
Mia said, *No, you are very old
and smell too much.*

The first time Mia spoke truth to power.

When Mother died, I sat with her,
watched her skin lose it's pink, turn to gray.
I combed her hair.

I touched up her lipstick,
took her rings from her fingers,
and thought the lure of grandchildren
was really the lure
of what could never be,
what flew from her grasp,
the little bluebird inside all our women,
determined to fly.

Things I Love—A Counting Poem

How the world can turn around,
    upside down, inside out
in an unforeseen second.

How often I forget that
    and am reminded,
for better or worse.

Counting the turn-arounds
    like looking back on the long trail
from the top of the high hill.
    Counting the switchbacks,
where the trail appears to disappear
    behind a pillar of tree or
looming boulder
    or over the cliff edge.

Counting the turn-arounds
    like falling in love at first sight,
long awaited pregnancy, unexpected diagnosis,
    and, of course, falling,
for better or worse.

Also, there are cats,
    alpacas, baby goats, fig bars, new peas,
halibut, and church bells.
    My daughter.
The sound of rain on the metal roof.
    Forget-me-nots and lily of the valley.
My daughters.
    Wild roses.

On the Seventh Anniversary of Her Sister's Death

I told my three-year-old daughter
her sister was alive in my heart.

She lifted my shirt
hoping to see her. *Oh my God,*

I thought, *What possessed me
to say that?*

This precious living girl
can't see anything except a black bra

and a swell of breast.
No sister there.

I remind myself that secrets
are salt on tree roots,

fire on skin,
poison in the pond.

This metaphor is truth,
just not to a three-year-old.

I can feel the warm morning air on my skin,
her peering face so close
I feel her breath.

Together on the red sofa
in the living room of the cottage
at the end of the dirt road.

Her sister invisible.

One More September Poem

In spite of the fact that Wednesday
is the thirty-second anniversary of her death
and melancholy falls on me
like a cape swirled by a troubadour
about to sing the famous song
I have heard a million times,

in spite of the fact that explaining
how much I still miss her
reveals a sadness as permanent as a tattoo
no one wants to see,

in spite of fact that my eyes have run out of tears
and feel like little gravel quarries,
and I know this is not merely a medical condition
common among aging women,

in spite of this,
writing one more poem about September
is a relief.

Sometimes You Have a Friend
For Sue

In the morning on the frost-coated field
when the birds fly up surprising you,
sometimes you have a friend
laughing beside you—
a brook of laughter between you
rolling through the air
that used to fill with the giggles of our girls—
our girls like young horses
all elegant manes and long legs
flying past us.

On the weekends when you take your daughter
to march against war, against gun violence,
climate sins and devastation,
sometimes you have a friend
waiting on a street corner with her daughters,
signs in hand,
and you march together.

On Monday mornings when the phone rings,
sometimes you have a friend
ready to talk,
to shake off the rumpus of a weekend with kids,
ready to enter back into the rank and file
of the linear working world.
Sometimes you have a friend
who calls every Monday morning
apologizing
even though you can't imagine
how else you ever started a week.

When the worst news comes,
the sledgehammer of a future
relentless with goodbye
in the slow fading of a worn-down mind,
sometimes you have a friend
who does not walk away.
Sometimes you have a friend who nods,
holds your hand,
who doesn't know what to say
and in not saying
is the one who holds you steady
through the long way out.

Sometimes you have a friend
who believes with you
that hope is a gift
without which we do nothing,
without which there is no first step.
We believe together
that our children are hope.
That we will find more hope together,
for each other,
for other people,
and we hold this like a flame between us.

Sometimes you have a friend who is a light.

Thirty-One

I woke with sadness like gravity
in my stomach.
I thought it was the state of this world,
the man in the White House,
the fires in California,
early blizzards in the Dakotas.
I thought I had finally been still enough for
these things to sift down through my heart,
to sit in my belly.
Then your morning email,
the sweet ritual of companions waking apart,
asked me how I was on this day,
the thirty-first birthday of my daughter
who died thirty years ago,
and I knew the gravity for what it is.

My body knows this day, even when my mind wanders.
You call me back to this, and I give thanks
for your attention to my life,
for her life,
for how my daughter is still my daughter,
how death do us part
is only one way of parting.

My Garden

Every year I am startled
by the flowers that make it through
the harshness of winter
and my neglect.
If you watched me in my garden
unwilling to stretch too far or bend too low,
noticing only randomly
what and how anything grows,
seeing my disregard for order,
you could imagine
I am a lousy mother,
leaving debris on the beds,
allowing unruly growth
and invasions of unwanted species.
My best part always,
looking up and saying,
Oh my God,
you are so beautiful.

After the Van Gogh Immersion
For Fred

Walking through the twenty-foot glowing screens
    of Van Gogh's paintings,
I thought about Cezanne.
    My loyalty to his black-trunked trees
whipped by wind,
    still constant after all these years
despite the glowing yellows and blues,
    despite the passion of Vincent's paint,
the brush strokes filling the walls and floor.

My lack of loyalty to the moment
    was a notice pinned to the wall
stating clearly how I was
    drifting like Manet's snow.

This isn't about aging or death
    or even cutting off an ear.
This is about immersion,
    letting memory flood in.

Like the moment I realized
    this person walking
through the door this night
    could be the father of my child.

How big the pause was then.

How I wish you could walk with me
    inside this Van Gogh painting,
watch our daughter turn and turn,
    like she did in her first snow, insisting
to go stand under the streetlight,
    looking up until her toes turned blue.

Van Gogh immersive experiences are real-life or
virtual reality exhibits of Vincent van Gogh's paintings.

Wedding Ring

The diamonds came from an old cocktail ring
maybe from the 1920s, a family piece.
When it arrived, it was so large
we set a place at the table for it
on a Delft-blue placemat. It resided
like a dowager aunt with a lorgnette
and a pillowy bosom that rested on the table.

We took the old stones and designed this ring—
the big stone cradled by the two smaller
in a twist, a wave of gold.
I have worn it for forty years
even though my husband's been dead for ten.
Last week when our first daughter
would have turned thirty-four,
I noticed one of the small stones was gone.
This little crater of emptiness
so graphic a reminder—
like a bowl I can pour tears into
that will never fill.
Yesterday I showed our living daughter.
She wanted to vacuum the whole house,
examine the debris with a magnifying glass,
sure it must be here somewhere.
I said—no, it's gone.
She said—Mom,
put your birthstone there.

For Lack of a Metaphor

Remembering my daughter's tutor, her swim coach,
women who taught her things I couldn't
even if I should have—
I wonder where my tutor, my coach is—
I mean right now, not when I was a kid
but now all weary and gray in another morning
washed with sadness.
I want someone to teach me a way through
I don't know. All my ways, tried and true,
well-honed and ready—I don't want them—
uninspired artist that I am—
all those colors and not a new one in that drawer
of expensive little tubes wrinkled up with use
like me.
I want someone to sit with me and drink
new wine in new skins and all of it really new—
not made of grapes or even fruit,
not a leather pouch or even an earthenware vessel—
all new and surprising and, of course,
wonderful.
When Fred died, I wanted a new car.
A new house. A new wardrobe. New food.
New love. Even new sex, sex beyond my imagination
and, of course, wonderful.
It's part of the disease of it.
The skin shedding discomfort.
The nothing fits right anymore of it.
So today I ask for the coach, the tutor,
and I get it!
Really.

My friend sends me a picture of a woman
in a woolly snowsuit, only her face exposed.
The suit is soft, glowy yellow,
emanating light,
and I realize
sometimes you can get what you want.

How to End Narcissism

If you, my daughter, were a beast,
you would be affectionate
with soft, curly fur,
long legs like a colt, four of them,
the intelligence behind the eyes decidedly human.

So, you are a mythical beast
probably with the ability to speak,
certainly with the gift of laughter.
You would be a beast of burden,
ready to trek long miles
carrying baggage and supplies
for refugees trailing a long line behind you,
children climbing up to rest on you.
At night they burrow in for your warmth.

If we imagine this for each other,
become magical beasts for each other,
we become so interesting,
no one will abandon anyone.
If mothers were charged with this exercise,
it would put an end to narcissism.

There are so many who need to be seen this way.

Let's imagine each other into newness
that still holds truth
like a clear glass holds sun and water.
Let's try this.
At the dinner table, ask
If Grandma was a mythical beast...

I can tell you, my sister
would be a large bird
floating on a blue lake,
her feathers blue and green,
her wingspan mighty.

Heart

There is a heart that is
neither a red billow on a page
or a pumping muscle.

Yesterday you stood on the deck,
Grateful Dead T-shirt falling off your shoulder,
ripped jeans showing your knees,
still tan from your trip to Mexico.
You talked about your work with
unhoused, hungry people.
I thought,
You have a lion's heart.

There's my heart.

The man beside me, not your father,
moved his knee up against mine
as though he knew I was, again,
stunned by you.
As though he knew
one day I would fall over from my wonder,
and he would prop me up.

There's my heart again.

This morning I write with my friend
who's name is a tree
that she looks like,
all lean and bendable,
her face shining through
new leaves.

This pen a heart.
Her face a heart.
This hour a heart.

The beat is all around me.

Notes from *A Distant Mirror*
From A Distant Mirror *by Barbara Tuchman*

On the best nights he read to me
from medieval history books.
Pages of battles,
boiling oil thrown over parapets,
severed heads trebucheted from towers,
my head on his shoulder,
I'd fall gently into sleep for hours.

He'd tell friends around the dinner table,
wine glasses blinking with candlelight,
a bloom of red wine on the tablecloth.
They'd laugh.
I'd pretend
to be sheepish at this exposure
of my tolerance for violence as a lullaby.
Mostly it was his voice, his heartbeat,
the burrow of blankets,
and across the room the shhshshh
of our sleeping baby.

I've told myself she never heard this.
Her grasp of words just beginning
like waves or wind in trees.
Now I wonder if this diet
of what we have done to each other
through all the deep tunnels of time
was her initiation into
this labor she gives herself to.

Let Me Give Thanks

Rain on the roof and ants on the kitchen counter.
My throat is sore. My neck is stiff.
I am alone, and my house is
cold from the night.
Stretching on the rolled up towels, I start my seven minutes of
breathing exercises, feel the stretch of tedious time
until the singing bowl on my phone app rings deep and long,
and I am so surprised that seven minutes moved through my breath
so quickly, and I feel my back as something more mobile than a board.
The heat clicks on.
There is hope for this day.
My daughter calls, crying, on the way to the hospital.
One of her thirteen-year-old clients was found this morning overdosed
with penises drawn on her arms.
Eventually she asks me how I am, and I say
I am a white, middle-aged woman, well-educated,
living in Portland in a dry, warm house.
She starts to laugh.

Sunday Dinner with My Daughter

We talked about cutting and Narcan,
trafficking and fentanyl,
seafood salad slipping on our plates.
A prawn shot across the table
when I cut it, we giggled,
and for dessert we talk of Maine,
pull our masks back on.
Precautions linger.

When she was born,
I never imagined this dinner
together in pandemic times,
her father dead for years,
our conversation so gritty and harsh
about this world she works in.
We both worry her soul will toughen
like leather in sun,
her heart will grow numb
like frozen fingers.
We speak to this, too.

We speak about following your heart,
finding brave work that mends,
finding moments in the work
where everything good
shines through.

We speak again of Maine.
An island that might have been made
for us to walk its rocky beaches,
stooping to gather the chips of shell,
the sun-catching stones,
to swim at high tide in the bay
loving how our arms, dried in the sun,
will taste of salt,

to read in rickety chairs on the front porch
before mosquitoes arrive
with the evening.

There are places we can go together
even when we can't travel,
where we know rest
and the soft coos
of mourning doves,
the drifting scent
of wild roses,
faded dish towels
flapping on the line.

One Piece of Broken Pottery

Short of a miracle,
my daughter, her friends,
don't imagine having children.
They don't see it.
Bringing children into this world on fire.

What can we say to this clarity?
This lack of optimism.

I want to offer
some small sprinkling of hope,
but none of it will put out the fire.
I could say,
maybe your child
would be the one to see
a way through this conflagration.
Or sometimes life calls us
even when it's beyond reason.

Every time I walk on a beach
with shards of sea glass and broken pottery,
the pottery is more precious to me.
The story goes
a woman would throw her best plate from a cliff
when she was sure her fisherman husband,
lost at sea, would never return.
These pieces, I'd think,
were pieces of broken hearts.

All I can think now is
I want to find
the one piece I have saved for years,
press it into her hand.

BLESSING

After all these years
I think of you first
Then I thank your father
And bless this house
Then I am on to me
Thank God I live alone at last

To Have Faith

that every peaceful breath
is a tiny reprieve
sent in my exhale of prayer
around the world.

> My breath,
> filled with clean air,
> quiet air sounding only
> of the mating songs of spring birds,
> this breath expanding and contracting
> my lungs and ribs through
> my pumping
> heart's red blood
> contained.

This is the question:

> How can this be?

How can this be action?
Prayer?
Significant?

And it is the mothers' question,
arms carrying children across
the cratered fields, rubbled streets
into lightless basements, caves, bunkers.

> How can this be?

> > And this be?

This thin string of faith,
we, who are not there,
have to follow now,
in this instant of this day
still gray with night and peace?

Awake in the Night

That feeling older than the hills,
maybe as old as the cave times,
maybe only as early as
waiting to be fed before Mother was ready
or knowing he had entered the dark room
    while Mother still slept
or wondering how the house
    so lively in light could be
    so still in dark,
wondering if I am the only girl awake anywhere,
wondering if when the sun rose,
    everyone   would be   gone,

Mothers, you know I was no unique girl.

You know the fears,
    now that I have mentioned them.
You know you can still wake in the night
    startled by your aloneness
and bring your full adult self
crashing into action,
turning on lights,
making tea,
finding a book to read
in which nothing tragic happens,
    and even then sometimes
    you wonder
where   everyone   is.

The dark begins to pale.
The dawn birds begin to call.
If you are lucky,
you remember you can pray
and give thanks you've made it this far.

Sometimes you hear in return
the worlds' hum rising in you,
the quiet reassurance
of the Great Companion,
and you say,
Louder, please

Screaming Without Sound

Somewhere someone you know

    stayed silent to stay alive.

      The hand on the throat,
the gun to the head,
      the knife, the muscle,

           forcing silence

                for one more day.

Sister, you've probably had this dream—

    you are being hurt

        and you can't scream.

Waking you look for the purple bruise,
           your blood spilling
    on the ruined sheets.

Don't pretend you don't know this.

Maybe it was even you
           swallowing something so wrong
    on the chance
           that right could return.

And when right doesn't come—

    break the glass,

    burn it down.

Let Our Anarchy Be First

I will stop soon.
Soon we will all stop.
Let's stop before they do.
Let our anarchy be first.
Let their laws no longer be ours.

We will be good at it—
if there is one thing we know,
it's subtlety, it's covert life,
it's hiding beneath the long skirts,
it's passing with our mothers' pearls around our necks,
it's hiding things deep, throwing the keys
into the swamp only we know the way through.

Once we were all bound—
if you want to argue,
just look back far enough—
there is never too far away a time or place
when you were not your own.

Let's go down to the sea,
meet there where the piles of driftwood
are our bones.
We all know how to get there
when we follow the maps below the maps.
Let's go there and build the fire,
bone by bone by bone,
light the night with this pyre
calling us in
one by one.

It's not safe here,
but it's not theirs.

Daughters, Listen
A message from the Great Mother

Listen, Daughter,
stand your ground.
I mean *your* ground, Daughter—
don't dig in unless it's yours.
If it's not, walk away—
no fight, no blame—
it's just not yours.
I wish I had told your mother.

When you walk away,
don't look back, Daughter.
Take your memories with you—all of them,
the pain, the joy, leave none of them,
but don't look back,
just promise the ones you have left
that they will go with you.
On your *own* ground, Daughter.
I wish I had told your mother.

If it's your ground, put your heart in it.
Don't be afraid.
If it's yours, people may be frightened
by your solidness.
They might dig up your ground,
wanting your heart,
but Daughter,
if it is your ground,
it will protect you, I promise.
Even if it seems nothing will grow here
with all their digging—
Daughter, it will again.

This ground that's yours
is deeper than they know.
I wish I had told this to your grandmother.

And Daughter,
I wish I had told your mother and your grandmother this—
your whole truth may feel dangerous,
but it is stronger than iron,
than diamonds, the sea.
It's the Fire in the Great Belly.
It's the golden thread,
clean air,
the secret of seed.

Live the Life that Chooses You.

These may be the wisest of the wise words
embroidered on my heart.

Sometimes I imagine the walls of my house
covered with framed wisdom—
calligraphed, cross-stitched, typed.
Perhaps this could be my last hobby.
Write them all down, line them up—
no better yet
let them crazy-quilt my walls—
a record of my learning.

I know you want to know what they say,
but I would like you to guess.
We can discuss if that is your wisdom or mine
but not until I'm dead
do you get to see them all.
Then you can imagine
the stories you know of my life
and see which wisdom applies.

You can take the ones you want.
Quilt your own walls.

Who Held You Through the Terrible Night?*

Sister, I imagine no one.

I imagine you alone on a hospital bed,
the drop off every time rushed and barely better
than being pushed, bleeding
out of a car barely stopped
in front of the glaring, empty emergency room
before there were armed and ready guards.

I see the pictures as though
someone was always cut out
or the details blurred,
numb with vacant gray.

I wish many other things for you.

I wish I was there, quiet, young,
tear-streaked, not knowing
but keeping my little hand in yours.
Faithful with you,
thinking there might be angels here,
somewhere, eventually.
I wish this story which is multiple
could be told this way to men
who still had room in their hearts
for light even when it hurts
because they, in the moment,
realize the full meaning of misbegotten,
finally.

They would fall on their knees
in front of all the mothers and sisters,
daughters and babies.

See us all as the angels we are,
with our swords finally unsheathed,
the cost of forgiveness again and again
beyond repair.

*Title from a poem by Judith Roche

Daughter of the Falling Star
A message from the Great Mother

     Tonight you think it is the end
The burning fire you shoot
                across the dark
a flashing trail the watchers
                want to last

     Night Wind Woman will whisper
               as you fall and dim
You are not separate, Daughter
We are all from the falling
    Lights

Now become another part of you
    blossom tree prairie sage rabbit elk
the salmon the whale chickadee red-tailed hawk
      or daughter or son
these sorts of being, too
              get planted by your fall
Your bright change
    always brings something new

      So, Daughter, your ending is a little trick
just because you can't be seen
    they think you are gone

     Some night around a fire
someone will ask
     Where have you seen a falling star?
The stories will start

    Where you have been
       changes everything

    If they look hard enough
  remember deep enough
            they'll find something new
began right then

Acknowledgments

This book flows from a confluence of streams, and I give thanks, a converging river of thanks, to my Quaker faith, the practice of Poetry Medicine circles with John Fox and my writing community.

Vashon Artists Residency gave me a month of quiet springtime, watching the light change on Quartermaster Bay. The huge file of poems I took there became this book. Forever grateful, Heather and Cathy. Thank you.

And I thank my mother from whom I learned so many important back-door lessons. And I thank Mia and Annalee for every step, every breath we've taken together. And Fred for being my beloved partner and the father of my daughters. And I thank the Irish grandmother I never met, and Edie, my grandmother who loved the intellectual life but not the farm.

My encouraging manuscript readers who also write with me: Birch, Meg, Esther, cousin Linda and David. Without your enthusiasm, thoughtful and generous sharing of your wisdom—no this. My coaches, my doulas, my teachers, my friends, I thank you.

And David, I thank you for walking with me through the hard work and all the rest and learning to love me as the stray cat I sometimes am.

Eric Muhr, thank you and your Fernwood colleagues for manifesting another dream. Your integrity overflows with kindness.

My sister, Kathy, my sister-friends, Sue and Terry, Pamela and Kristine, thank you for your willingness to hear the next one and the one after that. You are constellations in my dark sky.

And a huge thank-you to all my mother-friends. If you think you are in the number, you are. We can't do this without each other.

Title Index

A
   A Birthday Wish 10
   Advice I Wish My Mother Had Given Me 45
   After All These Years I Still Can't
      Believe You Bought That Plot 28
   After the Van Gogh Immersion 56
   Awake in the Night 70

B
   Baptism 32
   Begin Again 37
   Bench 19
   Blessing 68

C
   Cemetery September 2019 35

D
   Daughter of the Falling Star 79
   Daughters, Listen 74
   Do You Remember 43

F
Five Wishes 41
For Lack of a Metaphor 58

H
Heart 62
How to End Narcissism 60
How To Sing an Aria 39
How to Survive 16

I
If I Was a Shameless Hussy 20
I Thought You Were Dead 12

L
Let Me Give Thanks 64
Let Our Anarchy Be First 73
Live the Life that Chooses You. 76

M
Makeup 27
Migration Story 47
More Precious Than My Mother's Pearls 24
My Garden 55

N
Nectar 40
No More Imprint But My Own 11
Notes from *A Distant Mirror* 63

O
One More September Poem 51
One More Thing I Never Thought to Ask About ... 25
One Piece of Broken Pottery 67
On the Seventh Anniversary of Her Sister's Death ... 50

P
Please 14

S
Screaming Without Sound 72
Sometimes You Have a Friend 52
So Much Depends on the Frame 42
Sunday Dinner with My Daughter 65

T
The Best Solution to Some Days Is to Forget Them. 29
The Hum 34
The Risk You Take for Better 38
Things I Love—A Counting Poem 49
Thirty-One 54
To Have Faith 69

U
Unburying Angels 18

W
Wedding Ring 57
What a Mother Says 22
What I Really Want to Say 36
What Made Me Think I Have the Courage for This? 30
Who Held You Through the Terrible Night? 77

First Line Index

A
  After all these years 68
  A little crock of her ashes 28
  A sterling silver salamander 25

B
  Be faithful 18

C
  Check your breathing 16

D
  Do you remember that June in Harpswell 43

E
  Every year I am startled 55

G
  Get over it 22
  Grandmothers 14

H
  How the world can turn around 49

I

I am no longer my father's thing 11
I'd like to discover a book 24
If I had five wishes 41
If I was a shameless hussy 20
If you, my daughter, were a beast 60
If your mother knocked on your door 12
I lie on the hill above their stones 35
In spite of the fact that Wednesday 51
In the morning on the frost-coated field 52
I told my three-year-old daughter 50
I will stop soon 73
I woke with sadness like gravity 54

L

Learn to translate everything 45
Let me give you soft pillows 40
Listen, Daughter 74
Look up 36

M

My mother followed me across the country 47
My mother's lipstick was bright red 27

O

On a rusted metal tag 19
On the best nights he read to me 63

R

Rain on the roof and ants on the kitchen counter 64
Remembering my daughter's tutor, her swim coach 58

S

Short of a miracle 67
Sister, I imagine no one 77
Someday, I hope 10
Sometimes after a hard conversation 38
Somewhere someone you know 72
Start anywhere 37

T

that every peaceful breath 69
That feeling older than the hills 70
The art of learning to forget 29
The diamonds came from an old cocktail ring 57
The lurid purple and yellow fingerpaint 42
There is a heart that is 62
These may be the wisest of the wise words 76
This is the question that comes to each of us 30
Tonight you think it is the end 79

W

Walking through the twenty-foot glowing screens 56
We talked about cutting and Narcan 65
We think it is the sound of distant traffic 34
What if I really got it? 39
When you return to your home 32

www.ingramcontent.com/pod-product-compliance
Lightning Source LLC
Chambersburg PA
CBHW010046090426
42735CB00020B/3411